DIARY OF A BLACK WOMAN
MADEA AND ME

MARVA KING

DIARY OF A BLACK WOMAN

MADEA AND ME

MARVALOUS WORKS ENTERTAINMENT, INC.
GHETTOLECTUAL™ BOOKS
LOS ANGELES   2005

Copyright © 2005 by Marva King
All rights reserved under International and Pan-American Copyright Conventions. Published in the United States by Marvalous Works Entertainment, Inc. and Ghettolectual™ Books. No part of this book may be reproduced in any form or by any electronic or mechanical means including information storage and retrieval systems without permission in writing from the publisher, except by a reviewer, who may quote brief passages in a review. For information, contact Marvalous Works Entertainment, Inc.
11288 Ventura Boulevard, Suite 714
Studio City, CA 91604

www.marvaking.com   www.ghettolectual.net

ISBN 0-9770855-2-X

Manufactured in the United States of America

Dedication

I dedicate my diary to everyone who has worked in a stage production with Madea. I know we've all had some of the same experiences at one time or another. None of us could possibly have known upon becoming a part of the production what we would ultimately encounter. Although there were some good times on and offstage, the not-so-good times, the Tyler Perry tantrums and attacks, I still want to forget. I truly feel for those of you who struggle with issues of low self-esteem because you are the ones who were really tormented and ridiculed. I am and always have been a fighter, even if I do quiet, reserved battle. I defended myself on the *Diary* set with as much dignity, class, and respect for others as I could. Yet, it is my unwavering faith in the Almighty, the One who has blessed me with all that I am and all that I receive, which got me through the good, the bad, and the downright ugly times during the *Diary* tour. I pray that everyone affected by negative and confrontational forces use the shielding power that is given to us by our Heavenly Father. Putting that power into action, this diary is a one-two punch for us all.

Last, but definitely not least, it is imperative that I thank all my *Diary* fans. Thank you for your relentless love. Long after I left the cast, I was told by remaining cast members that your emails were positive and supportive, but unfortunately, they were deleted from Tyler's storyboard. I began receiving email on my website, www.marvaking.com, in January 2004. To those of you who attempted to reach me earlier and received no response, I am truly sorry. It has been great hearing and responding to fans who found me in the cyber world. I know how Miss Celie from *The Color Purple* felt when she read the letters from her long lost sister. It's fantastic. Thank you.

Acknowledgments

Special thanks to the Almighty who makes all things possible. Thanks to Theresa Goss and Black Insight Magazine, Inc., Keetha Lowe and Starz Entertainment - Bermuda, Gail Butler, and Roche Rogers for everything each of you did to help make this book happen. To Ty London: thanks for the memories. Sincerest thanks to the cast and crewmembers from the *Diary* tour.

Many, many thanks to Ronald Haralson, my mom Deloris Clark, my uncle Harvey Slayton and family, my son Darius, and my brothers Wallace and Terry Holcolm and their families—especially you Kayla—for your love and support.

DIARY OF A BLACK WOMAN

Introduction

When I first read the script of Tyler Perry's stage production, *Diary of a Mad Black Woman*—no, when I first read the <u>title</u> of the script—I thought, okay, this is probably an attempt by a man to interpret the emotions of a woman. I was right. In preparing to play Helen, the mad black woman, I pondered two questions: Who is Helen mad at? What is she mad about? The choices of people Helen has reason to be mad at are obvious: her husband, Charles, a cheater and a wife beater; and her friend, Brenda, who commits adultery with Charles. Exactly what Helen is mad about is not so obvious. Maybe she's mad because she's been faithful to Charles and tolerant of his ugly ways and because she trusted Brenda—her only close friend. Or, Helen could be mad because she's been stuck in the same pathetic cycle her entire married life:

Charles acts ⟲ Helen reacts

This is the pattern from the beginning of the play almost until the end. Running through the middle is Madea, Helen's grandmother, played by writer/director/producer Tyler Perry. Helen believes that without Charles she is nothing; absent some action by Charles that she would cease to exist. Her last lines in the script are a

DIARY OF A BLACK WOMAN

list of demands that speak of necessary changes in Charles' life although there is great need for change in her own life. Every sentence begins with "*You're* going to...." Some of Helen's commandments should begin with "*I'm* going to...." Helen is just setting herself up to react to Charles' next set of actions. Spiritual themes run throughout the play, but at times, Helen's faith in a higher power is fragile.

Charles and Helen dated in high school and have been married for nearly twenty years. Charles has been aloof for some time yet he is Helen's entire life. They have been trying to have a baby for the last seven years. Exactly what Helen focused her energy on for the first thirteen years is a mystery. I've always assumed those were the years when they truly loved and enjoyed each other; I never got an answer to my questions about that. The fact that they're rich and Charles is very controlling may explain why Helen has never had a job or many outside interests. Charles is a successful attorney with *too* many interests. Despite verbal, physical, and emotional abuse, even after Charles tells Helen he has initiated divorce proceedings, she does not possess the self-esteem and righteous belief that in return for twenty years of cooking, cleaning, and a sex life of diminishing satisfaction she is entitled to an equitable portion of Charles' assets. When Madea suggests that Helen should take Charles to the legal cleaners Helen meekly replies, Charles "established that law firm." She fails to realize that he did so while wearing clothes she laundered, eating meals she cooked, and sleeping in the bed she made. Mind you, this is no older woman going through a midlife crisis looking back at younger days and missed opportunities. Helen is thirty-something—in her prime years. At the end of the day, Helen is more depressed than mad.

I know that Helens truly exist. The reality is that we all have issues, but most women have a better grasp on reality than Helen.

I thought perhaps the key to understanding Helen is to examine the characteristics of the woman who gave birth to her. Exactly who is her mama? Fortunately, that is a question addressed in the play with clarity: Helen's mother is a God-fearing, church-going, hard-working black woman. She raised Helen to love the Lord and probably feels she married "well." Nonetheless, Helen partially blames her mother for her marital woes and goes so far as to suggest she approves of Helen staying in an abusive marriage so she can continue to support her mother and put her younger sister through college. Mama set the record straight right then and there: She turned her purse inside out letting every loose coin and dollar bill fall at Helen's feet. *Take the money, baby.* Mama made it known that she was living, breathing, and eating before Helen was born and would continue to do so with or without her help.

The plot continues along this path: Wealthy man tires of stay-at-home wife; inevitably, along comes the Other Woman and the grass looks greener in her pasture. At least, in this case, the other woman is over the age of twenty-one, but in all other respects she seems completely resistible. The action plods along with Helen vocalizing her plight until the end when, after a life threatening accident and being dumped by Brenda, in trifling dog male fashion, to Charles, Helen suddenly looks a whole lot better. Helen, however, takes a schizophrenic turn. She goes from docile and complacent to *kick-his-ass-'cause-it's-broke-down-and-book* mean. All morals go out the door. Her new attitude is clearly expressed in her response to the news that Charles may be near death: *"I hope he rots in hell."* Keep in mind that this follows a scene where Helen is down on her knees—literally—after being given divorce papers by Charles with Brenda as a taunting witness.

After Brenda excuses herself, Charles suggests he might stay with Helen if she will *"bark like a dog."* *"Ruff, ruff,"* Helen replies. Charles leaves anyway. After a few days of bizarre behavior that includes torturing Charles, who is now paralyzed and in a wheelchair by leaving him in the shower for three days, Helen *almost* leaves him for a wonderful, sensitive man; her bags are packed and she actually walks out the door, but then she realizes she loves her husband—a phrase she repeats several times throughout the play without reference to any attributes that make him even likeable.

There was a time on the *Diary* tour when certain people treated me like I really was Helen. I am by no means a mad woman, but after a while, I became quite annoyed. The opening

DIARY OF A BLACK WOMAN

scene of the play shows Helen writing in her diary about how miserable life has become with Charles. One night, when I thought about going onstage and pretending to write those dismal lines, I decided that I was going to begin keeping my own journal—the <u>real</u> diary.

Before I ever acted, I sang. I have sung songs I did not write, songs that do not represent my tastes, sensibilities, or me as a person. I have been required to bring life to dreams and fantasies that are not my own. Singing, in that sense, becomes acting. *Diary* truly is not my tale. I thought to myself, now I'm really going to have to act! Show after show, I became Helen by internalizing her characteristics.

. . .

Playing Helen is a part of my personal history. My diary is not a Tyler Perry bash fest; it is an effort to rectify my experience as a part of his stage production. There will be among my readers many diehard Madea fans. As to statements those fans find less than flattering, all I can offer is this: It is what it is.

January - June 2001

1

The Beginning

Dear Diary,

I know how privileged I am to get paid for being an artist, and to be able to stretch my wings by playing the lead role in a live theatrical production is a blessing, but playing Helen, the *not mad enough* black woman in *Diary of a Mad Black Woman*, wears me out. This is one of those nights when "mad" doesn't adequately describe the mood I'm in. Forget about the thick script I had to memorize and all the rehearsing I've done. Tonight, I feel like writing my own lines. I feel like going onstage and acting like a *natural* black woman. The audience comes to see Madea, but Helen makes a strong impression and at least half the audience leaves with love for her. The cast, now, is another matter. There are a few cast members who are a bit confused and need to understand the characteristics of a natural black woman. Then maybe they'll stop messing with me.

It all started when a Midwestern man joined the cast. Within days, he started telling other cast members I was trying to get with him and that he wasn't interested. Now don't get me wrong, the man is fine. The women in the cast talk about how fine the new man is and how lucky I am to have his attention and to interact intimately with his character. There's something about him. I can't put my finger on it, but like my mama always says, "All that glitters is not gold." So, I decided to keep my distance. Well, it should come as no surprise that a brother that fine is used to getting any woman he wants, and he noticed my lack of interest. He started telling other cast members I wouldn't stop touching him, and if I touched him one more time, he was going to punch me. Exsqueeze me! I haven't even considered giving him any play. Ordinarily, I would remedy this situation by just ignoring the brother until he gets over it. What some cast members choose to believe or disbelieve makes me no difference. They can spread all the rumors about me they want as long as they put a fine man in the mix to make the rumors interesting.

Oh, but this is some *other* madness. You see, there's this cast member who's jealous of everything about me, and when he (yes, I said *he*) hears the rumor that I'm trying to get with the fine new man, he (yes, I did say *he*) becomes very distant and competitive. Whatever. If dealing with a baseless rumor and working around the happy couple were the only problems I have on the *Diary* tour, I could work this gig for the next few years, but unfortunately, it just seems to get crazier and crazier.

In *Diary*, an emotionally and physically battered woman struggles through, and ultimately comes to terms with, issues of low self-esteem that render her powerless against her brutal, self-absorbed husband, Charles. The play starts with Helen, a docile stay-at-home

DIARY OF A BLACK WOMAN

housewife who longs to become a mother writing in her diary about the pain of being married to Charles, a successful attorney, who routinely ignores Helen's emotional and physical needs, and who she suspects of being involved with another woman.

Helen, in closing one of her diary entries, describes herself as "a mad black woman." Among the other characters are Daddy Charles, Helen's sly fox of a father-in-law, and Madea, Helen's grandmother and the comedic center of the play, both played by Tyler Perry. There's also Brenda, Helen's friend, an attorney/skank and the woman with whom Charles is having a secret affair. The action shifts between Helen's moping and whining about Charles' romantic apathy and Madea's slapstick, scene-stealing jokes until the end of the play, when life deals Charles a near fatal blow and Helen finally stands up for herself.

Portraying Helen has greatly expanded my range of characters. She and I are nothing alike.

Well, Diary dear, I'm glad I have you to release my frustration out in and to make note of things happening on and offstage. Writing may be the only way I'll make it to the end of my contract sanely. I think keeping a running account of what I'm going through will be therapeutic.

Anyway, now that I've let off some steam, I guess I'll go out there and play Helen. I don't know if I'm developing a higher level of respect or a greater resentment for this so-called virtuous woman. Helen is a caged bird, vulnerable and victimized, completely at the mercy of her cruel, vain, and selfish husband. One version of the ever-changing script even called for Helen to be raped by her husband. Diary, let me tell you something: If I ever write that I played a character who gets raped by her husband, before a live audience, I will also write that I punched my co-star in the stomach and kicked him in the balls—for real.

2

Getting to Know the Man Behind Madea

I first met Tyler Perry in December of 2000. We met in the lobby of the Doubletree Hotel in Atlanta where I was staying. The promoter of *Diary* was there to make the introductions. Generally, actors are selected and hired by the casting director, the producer, sometimes by a principal investor, or by the promoter. In this case, the promoter chose some of the principal actors. The hiring of actors, especially for lead roles, can become a power play. Any one of the players may feel he or she is the principal person in charge, the one who makes it all happen. The promoter provides the financial backing, and the producer and director provide the creative impetus that carries the production. It's a case of which comes first the chicken or the egg. My understanding is that the promoter wanted a certain look for the leading lady. Tyler hadn't hired anyone with that look. The promoter took matters into his own hands and hired me. Since it was the promoter who brought me into the picture, in this instance, he was the winner in that battle. Tyler took one look at me and said, *"You're pretty."* There was a certain longing in his voice that made me uncomfortable. It wasn't a "you're pretty" that suggested he wanted to get with me; I'm used to handling that kind of "you're pretty" without compromising my integrity. Nor was it the "you're pretty" of a confident person who is simply acknowledging beauty. There was something toxic about this *"you're pretty"* that, while I couldn't put my finger on it, let me know that I was in for trouble. The closest I can come to comparing the look he gave me with anything that is familiar to me is the look a woman gives you when you walk into a room with her man. It was as if he were a woman and this man, this promoter, who already had demanded that he use a leading character with a certain look had also brought another woman into his home, into his kingdom. *"Yep,"* I thought, *"I'm in trouble."* I didn't know why I was in trouble or what kind of trouble I was in, but I knew it was trouble. I later learned that as a matter of custom Tyler never hires a slim woman or actors who would take the focus away from him. He seems to hire women whose physical attributes don't bring out his own body insecurities. Otherwise, he won't be able to poke fun at them onstage. He made an exception on one occasion by hiring a friend from his hometown, but even then she played a confused, promiscuous woman with low self-esteem.

Now, it's very obvious that Madea is the real leading lady. From Tyler's vantage point, I did not exactly fit the Unattractive Female Lead mold. Yes, indeed, I was in trouble.

After our initial introduction at the Doubletree Hotel, we went to Tyler's home in a suburban

DIARY OF A BLACK WOMAN

area outside of Atlanta. A *real* mad black woman would reveal to the world the exact location of this home. While I'm sure the area has a name and qualifies as a town, it was way out in the boonies. Tyler had trees cleared from a piece of land and the house was built from the ground up. It was a big house, and cute. The house was simply decorated. Tyler told us that after the work had begun, snakes started coming up into the foundation of the house. They seemed to be coming from everywhere. The contractor had to bring in exterminators to get rid of them. I don't know much about snakes, but they generally flee into more wooded areas when grass and brush are cleared. It seemed strange to me at the time that snakes would be so at ease in an area that had been cleared for construction. I think Tyler has since built a larger, more extravagant home.

When we auditioned for the part, other prospective cast members and I read for Tyler from the *Diary* script and sang from our own repertoire. Overall, he seemed very nice. After the audition, we sat down and talked and ate junk food. It seemed that Tyler liked junk food a lot. As soon as I got the part, he began to exert unexpected control over my look. He selected wigs for me that I didn't necessarily care for, but they came with the job. I wore a Supremes-like wig for months before Tyler decided to let me wear a different wig. He also wanted my character to wear a fat suit, but I vehemently objected to that idea and was victorious. It's not, though, that I have anything against larger women. I believe that a woman of any size and shape can be beautiful. It's all in the way you carry yourself. Nonetheless, I don't think that any woman should alter her appearance to her detriment. For a slim woman to wear a fat suit is no less ridiculous than requiring a plus-size woman to wear a dress that is three sizes too small. Either way, the person looks like a clown. I flatly refused to wear a fat suit! Huh! How little Tyler knows about the female psyche. A woman's confidence and self-esteem are sometimes determined by her size, but insecurity and low self-esteem, and a willingness to accept abuse from others, is dictated from within and may be seen in a woman of any size. It was most unfortunate for us all to learn that Tyler dislikes his own body.

All physical and personality issues aside, Tyler is disciplined in his work habits. He reminds me a lot of Prince in that respect. Both Prince and Tyler do what they have to do to reach the desired result. Like Prince, Tyler insists that rehearsals and shows start on time and will work as hard as necessary to entertain the audience.

In the beginning, I learned that Tyler could be a cool person. However, as time went by, he began to go into diva mode. There were a lot of script changes within the span of a week's time. It seemed to really bother some cast members, but it was alright with me as long as I was left with enough room as an actress to do my job.

On opening night in New Orleans, Tyler's hometown, the house was packed. Tyler was

DIARY OF A BLACK WOMAN

back at home, back where it all started, and by "it" I mean the good and the bad experiences that make us who we are. That week the real Tyler Perry came out: the Tyler who has to be the focal point of every scene; the Tyler who might change the script on any given night to suit his whims; the Tyler who wanted me to wear a fat suit so he could improvise Madea's lines and call me fat onstage. If Madea ever comes at me like that, I will do a little script changing of my own. And it won't be pretty.

3

Helen

Believe it or not, the role of Helen was written for Millie Jackson. Millie had appeared in a different production with Tyler Perry in which she is said to have made major cheddar. For some reason, Ms. Jackson declined to play Helen. I would have loved to see Millie Jackson play the role. Based on her public persona, Millie and Helen are nothing alike. It would have been like asking Millie Jackson to play the wife in the movie *Fatal Attraction* starring Michael Douglas and Glenn Close. Not that Ms. Jackson is not talented, it's just that to be as docile as Helen would have required her to re-learn womanhood from an entirely different perspective. For Millie Jackson to take the amount of abuse that Helen takes and stay in character would have been something to see. It would have called for a performance worthy of a Tony, Broadway's most prestigious award, in a play not likely to be nominated.

I am under contract to play Helen for six months. Already, people come up to me on the street and call me Helen. I'm developing something of a cult following. The irony is that onstage, no matter how hard I try to become Helen, I never truly depict the character as she was written; I refuse to. I need to be able to breathe more feminine sensibility into my character, but I am not permitted to do so. One of the downsides for the cast, and an upside for Tyler, is that the writer, director, and producer are the same person: Tyler "Madea" Perry. There is no one to stop him from doing whatever he wants to do. The part of Helen was written to depict a weak, naïve, nonassertive woman until the end when she retaliates. During opening night of the play, the scene appeared where Helen was shown being raped and beaten by her husband. Over time, there were a couple of different women who played the role of Helen. When the rape scene was included, couples in the audience started to fight. Apparently, some women were reminded of sexual, physical, or verbal abuse they had suffered at the hands of their mates or some other predator. How uncomfortable it must have been to witness a woman being raped onstage, especially before a large church-going audience. It's a good thing that scene was stricken from the script forever! With scenes like that one eliminated, women and men alike love Helen. I believe a large part of what they like is the imagery, which is by far more fantasy than reality. Helen's life is some women's idea of perfection: a prosperous husband who enables her to be a stay-at-home housewife, a husband who takes care of everything, at least financially. Charles has placed Helen on a pedestal, which may sound splendid to some women, but, unfortunately, he seems to have placed her there and forgotten about her.

Once we left New Orleans and took the play on the road and we all saw how much people liked Helen, I started to have major problems. Tyler keeps trying to make me play Helen differently—more whiny and pathetic. I never said that I would not play her that way; I just never do. Silence sometimes roars. At some point, Helen should wake up and smell the coffee, stop taking her husband's crap and stand up for herself. Maybe Helen should get a job, or better yet, take some of her husband's bundles and start a nonprofit organization for physically and emotionally battered women. Helen and Charles were high school sweethearts. Charles graduated from college and completed law school, so there's a good possibility that Helen is a college graduate also. Yet, after twenty years of marriage, she's still sitting around the house all day, folding laundry. Love is sometimes said to be blind, but in Helen's case, love is nearly comatose. Helen seems to have completely lost most of her senses. She cannot <u>see</u> her husband for what he is; she can't <u>touch</u> him because he forbids her to do so. It's surprising that she can't <u>smell</u> another woman's scent on him. Brenda, Charles' outside love interest, looks like she reeks of cheap perfume. After what Helen describes as one hundred and sixteen days of barely speaking, she still has to ask her husband, *"Are you seeing someone else?"* Poor Helen. I, on the other hand, am in command of my senses, and I sense that some women in the audience feel about Helen the same way that I do. I sometimes hear agitated groaning. If Helen becomes any weaker, the women in the audience will hate her. I sometimes wonder in amazement, and I'm sure Tyler does also, why a woman as weak as Helen is so strongly admired by other women. I do try to bring comedy into the role so Helen doesn't evoke too much pity but, still, the love women show Helen is incredible! When I'm funny, if Madea happens to be onstage, she upstages Helen by saying something nasty or sarcastic that isn't in the script.

Helen is loved and loathed in equal measure. She is a character out of a soap opera, a woman whose sole responsibility is to exist, to dress up and respond to commands like a favored house pet. Just like a domestic animal, no one bothers to examine what's in Helen's head or in her heart until the end when her marriage is in shambles and appears to be past the point of reconciliation. But I suppose Helen accomplishes what was intended.

Although I am not fond of the style of my wig, it does serve as a shelter for my audio aid. Backstage, I sometimes have less than sixty seconds to get to my next entrance, so I was forced to devise a way to hide my cordless microphone amp box. Guess where I hide it? Yep, under my wig. To get it in place takes ten minutes of wrapping cord around my head and pinning and hooking the pack onto my own

DIARY OF A BLACK WOMAN

braided hair (which is breaking a lot of my hair out). Besides the fact that it makes my head look like an alien's, this technique does the job. (Well, there's no place else to put the mic pack unless I hold it in my hand!) All practicality aside, the wig I have is tacky. Why can't Helen have a curly 'fro or an updo? Then, I could hide my mic pack a lot easier, and those hairdos are in line with the times: Black women are finally coming close to getting over the hair issue. No longer is long, straight hair a status symbol among black women, not necessarily for the most progressive of reasoning—not because we've all come to realize that naturally straight or wavy hair is not "good" hair—but for a much more practical reason: Hair is now a mere commodity which may be purchased in various consistencies from bone straight to wet-and-wavy to downright country dirt road nappy. No longer must a black girl be ostracized because her hair does not grow long. We can buy any kind of hair we want. What's more, if a woman cannot afford human hair, the predominantly Korean purveyors of add-on and add-in hair make very good quality synthetic hair. No longer must hair length or texture be a source of either low self-esteem or arrogance among black women. Still, women should wear their hair to please themselves, not to conform to some standard of beauty that mainstream society has placed upon us. Some women look better with short hair. There's a certain actress who looks absolutely gorgeous with her cute, short haircut. I admire her as an artist. I am encouraged by her long list of accomplishments. I think, I'm not sure, but I think, she has reached a point in her career where, at least insofar as publicity is concerned, she can veto any hairstyle or outfit that does not complement her. So, when I looked up from my place in line at the grocery store and saw this lovely and talented actress gracing the cover of a major publication *wearing* some hair that looked about twelve times as thick as her own and equally as long, I knew she wore the hair because it was her desire to do so.

Where was I? I'm enjoying the writing process so much that I'll sometimes take the opportunity to sound off on things that mean something to me. Anyway, back to the play. I often wonder whether it's true, as I've heard, that Tyler based some of the domestic altercations shown in *Diary* on things that took place during his childhood. Tyler always talks about his mother and does a lot for her. Tyler has said that he was abused when he was young. I haven't gotten to know Tyler outside of the production. I don't know the variety of personality types he's attracted to, or how he treats his significant others. I've never noticed Tyler having a female date present on the set, but there have been a few persons who have come to see Tyler backstage.

> Speaking of hair, I'd better put this pen down and go wash my own. It's dry!

DIARY OF A BLACK WOMAN

Not long ago, a fellow cast member who had a thing for me was fired. He had some professional problems with Tyler. He was replaced by that fine Midwestern man (who was also eventually fired for undisclosed reasons). Had I been standing in the wrong place when the axe was swinging, I'm sure I could have lost my head, too. Well, I don't want to go. Why should I? I have a contract and an audience that loves me. It was suggested that I should either play a different role or leave the production. It was a lesser role for the same money, but, of course, I said "no," that I would neither change roles nor leave the production. As Helen, I may play dumb, but I'm not stupid. The problem is not my performance or my attitude. It's simply that Tyler doesn't care for me. Our dressing rooms are always right next door to each other. Everyone else is usually on another floor. Whenever our paths cross, if he says anything at all, it's a barely audible "Hi." Onstage, we both do what we have to do. Tyler will sometimes improvise and say and do things that are not in the script. Some cast members are thrown off by this. Most times, I give the sarcasm right back to him. When we get offstage, he screams at me and tells me to stick to the script. Other times, I just let him have his fun. After all, it's his sandbox. At times like that, I can't figure out where Madea ends and Tyler Perry begins. I have worked with Prince, Stevie Wonder, Michael Jackson, Anita Baker, Quincy Jones, Whitney Houston, and many others. (And no, Diary Dearest, I'm not going to write about those times.) I am well respected by my peers and former employers for my talent, my standards, and my work ethic. Without a doubt, working with Tyler is the greatest challenge I've ever encountered. If I were offered me a million dollars to do it again, I admit that I'd have to think about it, but even with a million dollars on the table, unless he has undergone a lot of therapy and has grown spiritually, I will not put myself in this position again. I'm sure I'm not the only actor who has come to this conclusion.

4

Madea Onstage and Offstage: More than Just Pretending

Dear Diary,

I realized something tonight: *Madea is the real mad black woman.* I took a good, hard look at Madea as she came offstage after the show. There stood Tyler-Madea with his/her hands still on his/her hips. That's when I started looking at the real man and the imaginary woman as one and the same. In the mad department, Madea has Helen beat. Let's face it; compared to Madea, Helen ain't all that mad. If Helen were a *mad* black woman, she would have cooked up a pot of hot grits and molasses and poured it on that Charles negro within the first twenty minutes of the play; just ask Al. Helen suffers verbal and physical abuse at the hands of her husband, and certainly, while domestic violence is as prevalent among black women as any other racial or ethnic group, the fact that a play could be written and successfully marketed, the title of which makes specific reference to mad black women, is quite telling. Black women have a demonstrated history that does not allow for the celebration of abuse. Within black culture, physical abuse of women is not the subject of comedy. Furthermore, I feel the play's ending is unrealistic in most instances. A woman as fragile as Helen would not have had the stamina to make such a miraculous emotional recovery. She would have had too many issues, been carrying too much baggage, to recognize, let alone almost hook up with, a good man within days of finally seeing her husband for what he really is. As if that isn't enough, my character, Helen, is really there for Charles, Madea, and everyone else to take their stuff out on. A man, Tyler Perry, plays Madea but one can't help but wonder if Madea is a wannabe woman pretending to be a man pretending to be a woman. In the end, could this be just a frustrated black man in a fat suit? The frustration we see oozing out of *Diary* is not something most women, mad or otherwise, can completely identify with. At its core, *Diary of a Mad Black Woman* is not about a woman who has grown weary of ill treatment by her husband.

Diary is about a lack of consideration and compassion, jealousy, envy, revenge, and, finally, forgiveness. With the exception of forgiveness, all of these emotions manifest themselves onstage in the physical and psychological battering of the play's female characters.

Charles treats Helen mercilessly. The suggestion is that he does so because Helen cannot have children, and in broader terms, simply bores him, but I think having a baby is more Helen's issue than her husband's. Charles goes on and on about how unhappy he is in their marriage, but never explains the source of his unhappiness. He suggests that Helen could never be the woman his lover is, but never articulates what he sees in Brenda that's missing

DIARY OF A BLACK WOMAN

in Helen. And how tacky is Brenda! It isn't her looks—Brenda is an attractive woman—it's everything else about her: her attitude, her demeanor, her outfits. To think that a man would choose Brenda over Helen, even in Helen's emotional state, is a bad joke. I think it was meant to be a bad joke. I think something else is going on here. I think Brenda is just a front. I don't think Charles likes women at all. I believe the brother is living on the down low and is leaving Helen for another man. Charles simply uses Brenda to force Helen to give him a divorce so that he can get with someone more likely to be named Brandon. Had Charles not had a terrible car accident, he would have left tacky Brenda in two weeks' time, and who would blame him? He had the perfect excuse: she's tacky. Charles would next have been seen with a man as meticulously dressed and manicured as he is.

> Remember to buy some pink nail polish. Buy pink lipstick? Maybe not, but look for something that goes nice with pink polish.

In developing the character of Charles, unless this truly was his experience, perhaps the writer took the physical and verbal attack on women a bit far. Charles doesn't just fall out of love with his wife. He doesn't just grow to dislike her; Charles cannot stand Helen. He can't even stand for her to come near him. What's more, pathetic as Helen is, with her folding-laundry-in-high-heels self, I think that Charles is envious of Helen. Partly, because Charles wishes that someone would take care of him while he walks around in fancy lingerie, and partly because the character of Charles, as it is written, demonstrates how a man who appears to have it so together really doesn't have a clue; if he did, he wouldn't be comfortable with the way he treats his wife.

Don't be thrown off by my perception of brothers on the down low. My view of *Diary* is not a commentary on the gay male prerogative. I do not believe that gay men want to *be* women. Of course, there are men who desire to *become* women. That's a different matter, and if they have the financial means to do so, they might undergo a clinical sex change. Other men choose to live a transvestite lifestyle. While some men, who either cannot afford the clinical procedure to become a woman, or who fear the stigma of being found out to be a transvestite, may be emotionally unstable because of their inability to live life as their true selves, Madea is none of the above. To associate Madea with any male person living an alternative lifestyle would be an insult. Madea is a freak. Madea loves being a freak. Is it just me, or are those boobies awfully big and perky for an elderly grandma? There are plenty of attractive, youthful-looking grandmothers, but Madea's breasts don't match the rest of the fat suit. They're perky, damn perky. Damn near torpedo perky. There is more than a small dose of vanity in that fat suit. How many truly elderly grandmothers shimmy-shake their breasts like Madea does?

If, as it is said, art imitates life, then what human characteristics or series of events could have come together to create Madea? What haunts the psyche of a man who truly wants to *be* a woman, and not just any woman, but a particular woman? Any number of negative life experiences during a boy's formative years could have been the catalyst: a child who has been raped comes to identify with women as the sexual victims of men; the primary male figure in this kid's life is physically and verbally abusive towards his mother—the primary female figure in his life, and the one who nurtures him—thereby creating an overall image of women as being overpowered by and defenseless against men. As an adult, the same person may develop feelings of inadequacy manifested in an inability to please a woman in the ways a man is expected to, or feels he might be gay by forced induction. Such a person may consider himself lacking in masculinity or attractive, if at all, in a feminine way. I can't help but wonder if some, if not all of these characteristics contributed to the mindset that allowed for the creation of Madea.

Clearly, Madea wants to be Helen. Yes, I said it, and as the woman portraying Helen, I have the goods to back it up. In choosing a woman to desire to be, Madea could have done a lot worse. Still, it's not a compliment. I'm comfortable in my own skin, and I'm most comfortable around people who are as comfortable in their skin as I am in mine. The Madea character does not resemble me physically. If Madea wants to be beautiful, then why—other than the fact that the character might have appeared too real and have been taken too seriously—wasn't Madea created beautiful? On second thought, why wasn't there at least an attempt made to portray Madea in a gorgeous Rupaul-like image and persona? The real Rupaul dressed and made up like a senior citizen would still look fabulous. Let's assume for a moment that it's not Tyler Perry in the fat suit, but rather, some anonymous wannabe woman portraying a man portraying a woman. Couldn't this be viewed as part of the down low syndrome? I don't think the audience would have found a man portraying a physically beautiful woman who spews venom and hurls not-so-subtle insults at other female characters the way Madea does as funny as a frumpy, lopsided wig-wearing granny. It would have been obvious that Madea is envious of women in general and Helen in particular. Instead, Madea is depicted as a grandmother who just so happens to have a sharp tongue. The majority of the audience either has, had, or knows a revered grandmother. Who cannot help but ask critical questions about Madea? Given the thoughts she expresses, not even years of living and acquired wisdom give Madea the right to say whatever she thinks. I must admit, while growing up in the hood in the Midwest I encountered many Madea's, especially after they'd had a bottle or two.

. . .

Madea's marital status and libido also defy a typical grandmotherly image. Is there so much as the suggestion that Madea could have a husband or a companion? I wish Madea had a male companion, 'cause she is one horny grandma! Madea has been known to run through the audience theatrically butt-naked (that is, wearing only the flesh-toned fat suit); she has grabbed at real men's crouches and sat and grinded in their laps. In one scene that was particularly irksome to two cast members who were real-life mates, Madea had a tendency to join them onstage during intimate moments. Why this grandmother figure constantly needs to exhibit perverse sexual tendencies is beyond me. Maybe she should hit the bottle and smoke a little chronic along with Daddy Charles and his friends; at least then she would have an excuse for being so horny. To many viewers, seeing a sexual component to Madea is funny because they can't envision her as a real person, but Madea is one psychotic *abuelita.*

Am I the only one who's ever wondered why Madea isn't shown making out with a nice, older man? Could it be that Madea is a front for the expression of the desires of the woman inside the man wearing the fat suit? How can a guy in a fat suit grab another man's crouch onstage and still claim to represent the sexual interests of women? Is the play's predominantly Christian audience truly expected to lose sight of the fact that inside the fat suit is a live-bodied male? Does Madea claim to be lewdly exposing a woman, or dreaming that the audience is really seeing her hidden desires on parade? To say that Madea is sexually ambivalent is an understatement. It would be no more surprising, from a psychological point of view, for Madea to run through the audience without the fat suit. In fact, it might appear more genuine. Any way you cut it, Madea is a freak; she is nothing nice.

Onstage, you can always count on Madea to improvise the side-ripping, slapstick jokes about other characters that make the audience roar with laughter. Most of these so-called jokes are not a part of the script. Sometimes, these jokes are added by Madea to take jabs at people Madea doesn't care for or has a bone to pick with. Sometimes, this seems to be the main reason such persons were hired in the first place. The other characters never know from scene to scene what they're in for. Madea has been known to point out a cast member's physical features that are not flattering. The unwitting audience finds this hilarious. Keep in mind that these cast members are not wearing prosthetic noses or lips, or makeup several shades darker or lighter than their own skin. When Madea attacks someone onstage, the audience sees her attacking a character, and in most cases, she's funny. I only wish he would take into consideration that he's actually attacking the real person playing the character and be mindful of the fact that the nose, lips, or skin tone the audience is laughing at are that person's real features.

. . .

DIARY OF A BLACK WOMAN

During my first night playing Helen, the audience went wild over my wardrobe. The "Oohs" and "Aahs" were endless. The wardrobe person had made all of these beautiful gowns for me. The next night, Helen was stripped of the attire that drew the most positive reactions from the audience and left with the less attractive dresses. Although most of the pieces are not what I would wear, the blue sequin gown would be nice to wear to a formal event. I've worn the same robe for months—a hideous green thing with sleeves that looks like they were made for flying. It's highly unlikely that any woman—at least in this country—would fold laundry in a robe like that one. Helen could lose socks up those sleeves. Not only are some of Helen's outfits hideous but as they get older they've begun to show signs of wear and tear from endless dry cleaning, but they're never replaced. Those in the audience with front row seats might see Helen in a different light; although she's a kept woman, she's not necessarily a well-kept woman. Maybe the women realize that Helen is wearing the same old ragged dresses, but the men in the audience continue to show strong signs of approval.

Interestingly, even when Tyler is playing a male character—Daddy Charles—he still manages to focus on the female character's looks. The men in *Diary* criticize other men for their actions, but they most often attack the women for their physical attributes.

5

The Understudy

The truth be told, *Diary* is a performance in what is known as the R&B Circuit. That's a step above the Chitlin' Circuit. The difference is not so much the quality of the production as it is the sophistication of the audience. The R&B Circuit attracts a more upscale clientele. The R&B Circuit's mostly African-American audience is made up of God-fearing, church-going folk who come to see *Diary* in droves. The majority of them have never seen a Broadway production.

The success of plays in this genre is based in large part on their use of religious themes and a heavy dose of gospel music. Yet, at times, the use of "worldly" content is mind-boggling.

Generally, there is no understudy in this level of theatre. At one point, it appeared to me that the role of Helen had been promised to someone else. Let's just call her The Understudy. I can imagine it being said that within a week I would bomb, with my no-real-acting-experience self. I met The Understudy during rehearsals in Miami. She was really nice. Tyler had a show running in Miami that was soon to close. We rehearsed in Miami during the day, and Tyler would do the other show at night. On opening night in New Orleans, The Understudy was nice only up until the end of my performance. When I came offstage, she didn't speak. That's how I knew I had nailed the part. Apparently, The Understudy knew that, too.

Written into my contract was the right to periodically take time off to work on my new CD. At one point, even though I was not recording, I was invited (or should I say, encouraged) to exercise that option. During my absence, an understudy had the privilege of performing. I thought, *be my guest.* I went to Los Angeles and South Beach, Florida, and I had a ball. Meanwhile, The Understudy was bombing. To make matters worse, Madea was really showing out, bashing the woman—who he had chosen—onstage. Madea just couldn't resist the chance to totally demean that person, in part, I think, because her looks made it easy for him to do so, and also because she was rendering such a poor performance. Cast members were calling me from backstage during the performance. They would hold the telephone so that I could hear the dialogue onstage. It was pitiful; I actually felt sorry for the lady. I stopped taking their calls.

I was away for one week. When I returned, there were hugs, cards, and gifts. Even Tyler seemed happy, or at least relieved, to see me. For a few days, he was pleasant. On my first night back, he introduced me as *"Miss Marva King."* I had never been introduced that way before. I knew then that the decision to try out The

DIARY OF A BLACK WOMAN

Understudy had been disastrous. Tyler seemed to have a new respect for me. I make what I do look easy—so much so that Tyler might have thought that anyone could do it—but believe me, it's not easy. I sometimes have forty seconds to get offstage, change clothes, and get to my next cue. Oh, remember that fine new man I wrote about, the one who said he was going to punch me if I didn't stop touching him? Well, he ended up getting fired. But before that happened, he ended up dating the guy who felt threatened by me on the down low. It was obvious to everyone. The two of them were always together, and the F.N.M. had puppy love in his eyes. After the show, a van would transport the cast from the theater to the hotel. Sometimes, the F.N.M. would be late coming out of the theater. When he finally came out the F.N.M. would just stand and stare at the man of his dreams with longing admiration. Meanwhile, we're all sitting in the van waiting for him. You could almost read his mind: *Please let me go with you.* Whenever he got lucky, those were the nights he didn't ride with us! Maybe there were new lines to rehearse? The cast and crew would ride back to the hotel murmuring in amazement. Those two were quite an item, which was cool with me, but a lot of the female cast members were sick about the whole thing. I just laughed. That's why you don't jump at everything that looks good. My only problem with the F.N.M. was that he was determined to try and make me appear incompetent. As it happens, his lover had a lot of influence over who got hired and fired in the production. There was a scene in the play where the F.N.M. was supposed to come onstage minutes after me. When I came offstage for my forty-second costume change, I would run off the stage to the top of the stairs where a wardrobe person would be waiting to dress me. I would literally start taking off my clothes as I ran behind the curtain and up the stairs. Instead of standing to the side, the F.N.M. would step in front of me and try to slow me down and make me miss my cue for the next scene. One night I nearly missed my cue. I ended up running down the stairs and onto the stage with my stiletto heels in my hands because I didn't have time to put them on. I had just enough time to click my heels in the air before landing on the wooden floor. I still made my cue, and the audience cracked up. I made the shoe routine a part of that scene, but I was still fed up, and I told the F.N.M. that from then on he would have to get out of my way and that I knew he was trying to sabotage my performance. About a week later, I found out he lied on me about touching him. Another cast member told me what the F.N.M. was saying. He couldn't understand what was going on, but I broke it down for him: it was a simple case of jealousy. The F.N.M. had a hard time watching me receive acceptance from the cast and crew and applause and praise from the audience. Maybe he wished he could play my role.

No one seemed surprised when Mr. Adonis got fired. During the time the down low dating was going on, one of them began to play a song in his dressing room—*There's a Stranger in My*

DIARY OF A BLACK WOMAN

House by Tamia—over and over and over. It was bizarre. He would play the song ten times in a row. I felt his pain. He was either sick in love or a Tamia fanatic. Either way, I wanted to scream. That crazy episode just reinforced what I already knew: If you're going to date someone on the job, try not to date (a) people you work with; (b) the emotionally unstable, (c) people with short attention spans, or (d) those who exhibit the traits of all of the above.

MARVA KING

> **NEW SONG IDEA:**
> *"Sensuous Man"*
>
> *There's one kind of man who lets you know he's a man. You just understand that he is a man. He walks like it and he talks like it and he, he looks like it and he, he smells like it and he got skills, keeps it real, gives me chills, can you feel what I'm saying? I can build my life with his....*

6

Shaking Things Up Behind Stage

Since I returned from my brief vacation, things have been okay offstage, but onstage there are still moments when I want to charge Madea. Even as a fictitious character, Madea has mental issues. At one time or another, Madea is a monster toward everyone. I have never allowed anyone to treat me badly. It hasn't taken long for Madea to see that if she does things to me I will retaliate with diplomacy. If she changes the dialogue in the middle of the scene to take a shot at me, I'll shoot a dagger right back her way. I'm not supposed to know how to ad lib, but I learn quickly under pressure. I even have fun in the battle. If Tyler approaches me offstage about something I've said to Madea that isn't in the script, I go into another role I've mastered: dumb blonde. I give him an innocent look and say, *"No, Tyler, what are you talking about?"* I act totally puzzled over whatever he says I've done to Madea. I think Tyler realizes that I will do battle either with Madea or with him. I think I'm convincing in my denial of Tyler's accusations because some cast members believe me. Others chuckle about it with me later. Now and then someone will tell me that Tyler complained to him or her about the things I do; I don't care, and they understand. By now, most of them realize what's going on. I

DIARY OF A BLACK WOMAN

believe Tyler sometimes feels that maybe he's being unfair to me, that he really has no reason to dislike me. Most of the women were catty and distant towards me when I first joined the cast, and several of the men tried to hit on me, but as they saw that I don't have the attitude they were accusing me of having, they came to me one at a time and said that at first they thought I was this way or that way, but that I'm a cool person. Cast members have told me that they are amazed at how I handle Madea and Tyler and that they have a lot of respect for me. I just say my prayers. I am not going to let anyone destroy my confidence and pride in who I am and what I'm doing. The devil IS a liar! But I have to admit, there are days when I wish it had been Madea instead of that fine new man who had threatened to punch me.

I'm an only-girl. I grew up having to stand my ground against my brothers, and I got good at it. On my worst day, I could wear Madea out. Part of me feels sorry for Madea, but another part of me can't stand how she continuously searches for an opportunity to DESTROY another human being. I would love to get into a boxing match and punch her in her fake chest and snatch her wig off *Jerry Springer*-style.

> Relax! Only three hours left until curtain time. Light some candles and take a bubble bath.

As Tyler sees that everybody else likes me, he's started being nice to me and inviting me out as part of the group. I don't know if he is genuine or if he just doesn't like being left out. We've been getting along okay, but now we're at the very end of the tour, and it appears to me that the promoters don't want to pay some of their debts. It's gotten way out of hand. Everybody is arguing and fighting with the producers and promoters. They've decided to tape the play and promote the performance on videocassette. That should be good news to the cast, but the plan is to not pay more than $500 per person, including me. Even though acting is relatively new for me, I know that those tapes might someday be for sale at every live performance venue, video outlet, Christian bookstore, record shop, swap meet, bootleg warehouse, and Big Momma 'nem garage which translates into royalties a/k/a money-I-could-collect-for-a-very-long-time. I've been in this situation plenty of times in my recording career, and this time, I'm not having it. Most of the cast seems to be going along with the program; they're saying that they will perform for the taping with the full knowledge that they will be paid $500. Some have expressed the opinion that if they don't, the producers will never hire them to work in another play. I say, what the heck. This is my first play, anyway, and I've been supporting myself just fine for years. I see no need to sell myself short.

> Call Darius.

I think most everyone has accepted $500 except me. Someone suggested to me that I

… perform for the taping but not sign any agreements. I know from the music business that without written consent, the production company won't be able to release the video.

Guess what? The taping is over, but here's what happened: The promoter kept saying that he was going to pay me back monies that I'm owed for a few shows. Had I simply held my breath, I wouldn't be writing right now—I'd be dead. On the day of the taping, I decided that I was not going onstage without my pay. Tyler saw me, and I told him the same thing. I gave two hours' notice: either I get paid in full or I would not go onstage. They had six cameras in position, everyone else was ready to go, but two hours passed and I hadn't been paid, so I held up the show for fifteen minutes. A Tyler Perry production never starts late! This prompted the promoter into action. He wrote me a check and I went onstage, but that was not the end of the drama. I had been told that they were taping one performance, but they actually planned to tape two shows. I had gone out to eat with a friend of mine, Cherrelle, during the break. When I got back, Tyler was in a panic. He thought I had gotten my back money and quit. He had been blowing up my cell phone. Meanwhile, completely unaware that we would be taping another show, I was having lunch complete with a couple of glasses of wine. Onstage during the second taping Tyler was pissed. Backstage between his scenes I'm told he threw a tantrum, clowning something terrible. Someone told me that the rest of the cast watched my performance on the monitors and commented that I was doing well. The same someone told me that Tyler gave his worst performance ever. It was not my best performance; had I known about the second taping, I would not have come back full of food and drink from my sumptuous lunch. I felt tired and sluggish; my belly was bulging. We all knew that Tyler wouldn't use the second tape. Yet, despite his own mediocre performance, Tyler did use the second tape. Damn! Neither Tyler nor I look or perform as well on the second tape as on the first. That's when I formed the opinion that Madea and her madness were invading Tyler's brain. Why he would make himself look bad and put the video at risk just to spite his least favorite cast member? Mine was not a stellar appearance and I've looked better, but neither my performance nor my appearance was bad enough to be worth what Tyler stood to lose.

> **DATE TONIGHT!** Wear black or beige dress? Wear hair up?

As for royalties, I'll probably never get any, but at least I got all of my back pay and a substantially greater amount of money than the promoter had planned to pay, which everyone might not be able to say. I look at it as one of those times when you're up against an undefeatable foe, but at least I didn't just lie down and take my beating.

7

Connections, Kisses and Misses, and Getting Conked in the Head

Dear Diary,

Today my mind is full of disassociated memories of embarrassing incidents onstage. It's like looking into a kaleidoscope of *Diary of a Mad Black Woman* moments. It's surreal, as "Hollywood" loves to call every experience they have these days. I expect to turn on the television any day now and hear someone refer to their latest trip to the toilet as *"surreal."* Maybe I'm having after effects from a blow to the head I took during one of the performances. I'll see if writing down some of these random images clears my head.

Mama Dearest

Everyone thought the first person hired to portray my mother wasn't a very good actress. I thought she was a good singer. The problem was that the role called for a conservative look and she wanted to look as glamorous as Helen. Her competitiveness, on and offstage, got her fired after only a few weeks. A couple of times the makeup artist had to tell her to get out of the makeup chair so he could make me up first. I go onstage first and my makeup job is more detailed. Helen is a glamorous, rich housewife, for crying out loud! Tamela Mann was hired to play my mother next. She was great, absolutely believable right from the start. I found myself truly embracing her as my mom onstage.

Oh, My Aching Head!

Curtis Blake, who plays my husband, Charles, has been very helpful and encouraging. He knows this is my first play so he gives me pointers and tips backstage. I appreciate him very much. People who have seen the play are starting to write in to Tyler's storyboard about Charles and Helen. Many women are annoyed at Charles' behavior. Curtis is becoming more and more affected by the comments and is starting to verbalize his displeasure to other cast members. I never look at the comments. I don't even own a laptop computer. So I just do what I do onstage, totally unaffected by the audience's comments. Well, not Mr. Blake! Last night when I was doing my bark-like-a-dog routine, when I grabbed Curtis' ankle and began to grovel and plead as I do every night, he snatched his leg back with a little added aggression and kicked me in the head. He caught me in the temple with his knee and I almost lost consciousness. Not noticing that I was hurt, Curtis walked out the door as usual. From the orchestra pit and the first few rows of the audience it was obvious that I had been hit for real. Band members gasped. But people further back in the audience probably thought that it was a routine part of the performance. Well damn it, it wasn't. That really hurt! Later, I told Curtis to chill out, that if something like that happens again, just as he starts to make his cocky stroll out the door, I'll pound his bunions with all my strength.

I Just Felt Like Being the Big Dawg

I usually bark like a Chihuahua when I do the doggie scene, but during the second taping of the video version of the play, I jokingly barked like a German Shepherd. Oh boy, with my luck, that version will be the one released for sale! That wasn't the only time joking turned out to be embarrassing. In our first scene together, I cry when Charles leaves the house after telling me he's not happy. The script calls for me to make gestures as if I'm begging and pleading with him. Since the band would be playing, I always thought my microphone was off and to amuse myself, I'd cry in a silly, play-crying voice. When I heard those sounds on the video I could have cried for real. I guess that's what I get.

The Kisses that were Supposed to be Misses

During our romantic living room couch scene, my love interest, Orlando, was scripted to <u>almost</u> kiss me. It was supposed to come off as one of those uncomfortable moments when newly attracted people who haven't quite reached the kissing stage are nearly overtaken by passion but they catch themselves before their lips touch. In our case, the band sounds a telephone ringing that jolts us out of dreamland and back into reality. There were a couple of times when the band intentionally delayed ringing the phone and rather than leave our puckered lips hanging in midair, Orlando and Helen would have to go ahead and kiss. Afterwards, down in the orchestra pit, the band would get a big laugh and my make believe lover would smile. That actor is in my opinion the most handsome man on the stage, but I'm not trying to improvise and kiss anyone unscripted. I have to admit that there were times when we were cuddling and flirting onstage that I truly felt steam rising, but we were just in the moment. It never went past the stage.

Oh, alright, so I did have a casual dinner date with the man. In fact, I had dinner with both of the men in Helen's life—Charles and Orlando—once each. Although he was very nice and polite Curtis (Charles) was a very conservative spender; we went Dutch. Cordell

(Orlando), on the other hand, was true to his character. He was generous and giving and invited me to a more expensive restaurant and paid for my meal. If they were to read this it probably would be the first time either of these gentlemen learned that I had dinner with the other. For what it's worth, I found Cordell a bit more interesting than Curtis and I believe we both had intentions of furthering our acquaintance. (Just in case this diary slips into the wrong hands, I'll just leave it at that.) For the record, I never went out with either one of them again.

. . .

Don't Play That Song Again

I hated the video production's original music, most of which was written by Tyler Perry. During my six months, there were other songs that were at one time included but were taken out of the videotaped version. I don't know why; maybe because they didn't acquire the necessary licenses to release that material on video. There were two songs that were really effective—an Al Green song that played during the scene when I enter the set after starving Charles for a couple of days and a George Clinton song when Madea and Helen attack Charles in the wheelchair. We really got our ghetto gangsta groove on to that song and the audience roared with laughter.

I Can Bring Home the Turkey Bacon *and* Fry it Up in the Pan

When I first joined the cast, everybody thought I was one of those green grass-only eating heifers. They would constantly make comments. I'd just laugh and deny it. Tyler even occasionally made references onstage to me not eating or cooking. I was born in Michigan but both of my parents are from Arkansas. Need I say more? I've been cooking greens, yams, fried, barbecued, baked and however chicken, cornbread, and making homemade ice cream, cakes, and pies, since I was in elementary school, and word to my Moms, when we stayed in suites with kitchens, they soon learned this. On one particular grocery-shopping trip my cart was filled with ingredients for soul food cooking. "Are you going to cook that?" a band member from the South asked. Duh! Did he think I was going to pay a hotel employee to cook it for me? He said he'd heard I only eat salads and grassy stuff. I guess he believed it. Once I made my special apple spiced rum muffins with real 120-proof Jamaican spiced rum. Many cast and crewmembers swore they got drunk from eating them. One person claimed she was such a Christian that she couldn't possibly try one. What do you know? Tyler heard about my cooking and started talking to me about nutrition, staying slim and his misconception about my eating habits. I told him that I use a lot of natural ingredients that digest in your system quickly and easily, and that I could help him with his diet and exercise regimen. We never got around to doing that. I really hate that our near-rapport was destroyed by misunderstandings and professional competitiveness. I would have liked to really get to know Tyler and for him to know who I really am. What I learned about Tyler is that he seems to be much less an extrovert than the Madea character. The real Tyler has a rather reserved, almost bland personality. Besides having a quick temper and a sharp tongue, Tyler appears to be the total opposite of Madea. It's as if he created Madea to allow himself to release his pent up aggression and hidden emotions.

8

It's a Fight!

As a kid I walked to and from school in the Winter, Fall, and Spring. Nothing was more exciting than when a kid looked out of the classroom window and screamed, *"It's a fight!"* Fighting at school meant getting suspended, and where I grew up, in nearly every household, getting suspended meant getting that butt beat at home where there was no fighting back. But for some reason, the route to and from school was outside the jurisdiction of the authorities in our young lives. It was a gray area—no one, not school officials, parents, or students—was sure who was in charge of us kids between the time we stepped off the school grounds and the time we walked into our respective homes, and as a result, that space was neutral ground for mischief.

The slightest provocation could result in a fight: you bumped into someone at recess, or someone "heard you were talking about them," and it was, *"I'ma git you on the way home."* If you were the one who was gonna get got by the school bully, you might try a defensive pose, and if that failed, you might stay late after school and help the teacher, but not all of our teachers were sympathetic—especially the males. Some were either sadists, and glad to see some poor kid scratched and pummeled, or one or both of the particular kids involved were such troublemakers that the teacher was glad to see either of them take a beatdown. Those were the kids who stuck their tongues out at the teacher, made comments about his gut, his crater skin, or his bald spot; the ones who noticed those funny-looking, sometimes oozing lumps on the back of the teacher's neck, where hair didn't seem to grow, and asked, *"What's that on your neck?"* Kids can be cruel. If you were the one about to take a beatdown, you might give the teacher a pitiful look, hoping he has amnesia about what you said just the other day, but in response to your plea for sympathy and your facial expression of fear, he growls, *"Go home."* As if he owned the classroom.

Fights always seemed to break out way before or way after my house. I would hear the primal scream, *"It's a fight!"* and like a pack of wild animals, everyone would become aggressively stimulated. Every kid walking home would suddenly change routes. We would all run in the direction of the fight—ecstatic, euphoric, adrenaline pumping.

Similar to the route home from school, backstage on the *Diary* tour, and generally, any offstage area, is sometimes neutral ground for unsettling and extremely childish behavior. One night a while ago, far away from our present production of *Diary*, while I was in my dressing room getting made up, a crewmember told me about a situation that occurred while he was working in a different production at the Beacon Theatre in New York City.   I believe his story, because he began by telling me something I know to be true: that Tyler is never late for his curtain call, nor does he tolerate lateness from anyone else. The crewmember went on to say that on that particular night, Madea missed her curtain call.   Everyone was shocked.   A couple of crewmembers started to search the theater. One of them even ran to look outside.   He noticed people looking toward the alley that led to the backstage door. Low and behold, there stood Madea, as bold as the Statue of Liberty, fists balled, wig bouncing back and forth, arms flying, mouth spewing venom. She was throwing down, going toe-to-toe, or should I say, head-to-waist, with a five foot FEMALE crewmember who happens to be working with us right now on *Diary*. She's very feisty and controlling, but she keeps things rolling around this camp. I picture this St. Bernard doing battle with a Chihuahua. I heard the big dog did more barking than anything else and the little dog was leaping up to swing at the big one's head. I am overtaken by that old childlike excitement. That childhood chant—*"It's a fight!"*—rings through my head. Boy, does it bring back memories. For a moment, I'm lost in fight mania and I have mixed emotions. On the one hand, I feel like a man should never hit a woman, but from what I understand, this particular woman was the one who invited the man outside. On the other hand, if he fights men at all, I bet this big dog is a lot more selective about the height and weight of the men he fights.

Still, I applaud a senior citizen who defends herself. *"You go, Madea. Don't let that young girl beat you down."*

I've heard stories of more than one fight during Tyler's productions. Once, Ty London who plays Willie, Daddy Charles' old friend, and Curtis Blake who plays my husband were backstage during a show. They sometimes had as long as twenty minutes before they were needed onstage. Curtis said something to Ty. Ty responded in a retaliatory manner. Curtis threatened to hit Ty who is shorter than Curtis, slightly built, and appears to be soft, but Ty responded with conviction: *"Bring it on!"* A surprised Curtis backed off. Later, he told me, with a chuckle, that he backed off because he realized Ty, who Curtis considered no match for him, was prepared to take him on.

When *Diary* was running in the Midwest, we had a day off. We checked into a Marriott Courtyard sometime between 1:00 and 2:00 in the afternoon. There were several restaurants and bars nearby. Usually, I opt to stay in my room and rest and have quiet time. But at 8:00 in the evening when two cast members, Ty and his good friend who plays Brenda, my so-called girlfriend, knocked at my door, I let them in. They had just left a bar and proceeded to tell me an amazing story about some of the cast and crew who had obviously had too much to drink. The brother who plays Orlando, my love interest, who has a short fuse and is known not to take anything off of anyone, had a confrontation with

DIARY OF A BLACK WOMAN

the makeup artist. Earlier in the day, Ty's friend had become offended because of some remarks made by my short-fused love interest. Later on, just to spite her, he offered to carry my bags into the hotel lobby and held the door for me, but did not extend the same chivalry to her. As the drinks flowed, she began to attack the brother verbally. He had to be restrained from attacking her physically. Fortunately for Miss Thing, he didn't hit her; I was told that in another production he spanked a female cast member kinda bad. Although the man is nice and sweet to me, I see that he is as thuggish and gangsta as that original fine thug I recommended to play Orlando. (My thuggish friend was hired then fired after one week; I'll tell you more about that later.) The crewmembers left when the ruckus started. The restaurant manager put the remaining cast members out of the bar. Alcohol and pent-up sexual tension probably played a big part in that eruption.

I heard that in an earlier stage production the two men hired at separate times to play my love interest in *Diary* got into a fist fight—onstage. For the sake of clarity, I'll call them the Second Orlando and the Third Orlando. The Third Orlando is said to have beaten the Second Orlando to a pulp. The audience thought the fight was written into the script until the Second Orlando was thrown through the wall of the set.

And they say hip hop is violent.

DIARY OF A BLACK WOMAN

> Get your butt up and work out in the morning!

9

My Real Name is Marva

Hello Diary,

It just occurred to me that I never formally introduced myself. My dad's cousin named me Marva. I was born in Flint, Michigan. When I was seventeen years old, I moved to Los Angeles, alone, with $250, a one-way plane ticket back to Flint, and a dream. My parents were professional musicians, so music is in my DNA. My dad is deceased, but mom still sings.

CALL MOM

I've been singing almost as long as I've been talking. This acting thing is another story. I was not a child actress, nor did I ever aspire to become an actress, but I've caught on quickly. That might be because I've seen plenty of drama in my lifetime, and a fair share of comedy, so I have a large store of memories and impressions to draw on. I've been through a lot of stuff, but let's separate fiction from fact: Playing the role of a mad woman doesn't come naturally. I guess I'm just not all that mad. Actually, I take issue with the title of this play. Why isn't the play simply called *Diary of a Mad Woman?* What's the difference between a mad woman, in general

DIARY OF A BLACK WOMAN

terms, and a mad *black* woman? Well, no, I take that back; there is a difference: I think it's all the extra things a black woman displays when she's mad. The only logic I can draw from the title is that someone knows that some men can really get to the core of some black women's nerves. Since that is the case, the play should be titled *Diary of a Woman Driven Mad by a Black Man.* I could come up with a million alternative titles.

How, you might wonder, did I get tied up in this ineptly titled production? Well, there I was, minding my business, when along comes Tanky, a friend, with a bright idea: "Marva, you should be an actress." I had been working as a singer/songwriter/producer all of my adult life. I'd had a few speaking parts as a featured extra on television shows, mostly monosyllabic utterances, mere body movements, or facial expressions. I have written music for sitcoms and movies, and would sometimes be asked to audition for parts. I managed to attract the attention of a theatrical agent, which is not easy to do, and I took a few acting classes, but I wasn't terribly interested.

> Book studio time for next week.

I have been involved in music projects since elementary school. I've been in the music business since high school. I have enjoyed success and endured failure. The source of my success is simple: The Lord's blessings and God-given talent. The source of my failure not as simple: I'm a nonconformist. I sing the styles of music that I want to sing; I don't do drugs; people in high places don't do me; and I don't brownnose. I have been presented with and lost countless opportunities because I refuse to compromise my values. It happens over and over. Through every disappointment, I stick to what I believe and keep going. I'm happy, and I've remained optimistic. By the grace of the Almighty, the opportunities keep coming.

Now that I am a seasoned artist, I realize that all of my trials were to make me into the incredibly strong and wise woman I am. *"To whom much is given, much is required."* Now, I can see the value of the knowledge I've gained.

Lyrically, I have a lot to say and I have a lot to pass on to the young females coming up in this industry. I also have acquired a wealth of music and business knowledge and strategies that I apply to my own career.

> **Call Nio about lunch on Monday.**

Tanky is significantly responsible for my accepting this role in *Diary*. He called me and told me about a leading role in a stage production. I knew little about stage productions and nothing about Tyler Perry. I told Tanky I would give it some thought and get back to him. I had an opportunity to record a CD under the

DIARY OF A BLACK WOMAN

guidance of my new manager who also manages the Baha Men *(Who Let the Dogs Out?)* and a popular jazz saxophonist. There was an offer from a label in New York. If I did the play, my recording schedule would suffer; I really had to give this some thought. Tanky left me messages for two weeks. He was persistent! He said this was something that would *"change my life."* Listen, I'm in the music business. In my industry, that line is as common as a man asking, "Don't I know you from somewhere?" For two weeks, I didn't return Tanky's calls. Still, I found it ironic that I ran into him that day at the airport in Las Vegas. We both were in a hurry, but I know this happened for a good reason. Tanky finally got my attention: He told me that Tyler Perry's play was a musical and that I might be able to sing a few of my original songs in the production. Now I was interested. I auditioned, got the part, and negotiated a contract that included acting and songwriting. Unfortunately, the songwriting provisions of my contract were not honored, but I am permitted to sell my music CD and merchandise at the performances. At every performance of *Diary*, I make an effort to befriend the audience and I autograph pictures of myself. My CDs and t-shirts sell fairly well. At the end of the day, I think it's the admiration shown my character by the audience that makes this rocky road worth traveling.

I wanna ask you something. Do I appear vain? I'm really not. Black women are beautiful.

DIARY OF A BLACK WOMAN

The woman who plays my mother in *Diary* is beautiful. Why must we wait for someone else to tell us what we should already know? I have a friend who grew up in Jamaica. She's very pretty, and very dark-skinned. Growing up, everyone thought that her sister was the cute one because she had caramel-colored skin. My friend has a tremendous amount of self-confidence and she's crazy, in a good way, always cheerful and upbeat. She said that when they were little girls and people would go on and on about how cute her sister was it didn't affect her in the least. She said, in her Jamaican accent, *"Chile, I didn't care what other people thought, because I knew what the mirror was telling me."* Ladies, love yourselves.

10

Meet My Friend, Ty

Dear Diary,

How rude of me not to introduce my friend, Ty London, who has helped me through this madness. Ty is also in the cast of *Diary*. He plays Willie and the male nurse. Some of what I've written are things Ty and I commiserate over. I introduced Ty and one other actor to the promoter, and they both were hired. The other actor is a very good-looking man. Half of the women in the cast were looking, and...wishing.

So were some of the men; but this guy is a true thug. He immediately made it known that he is true to straight, thug life, and, what's more, that he was not taking anything off of anybody, the director included, and that his "people" were not to be treated or spoken to rudely. And I was his people. The next day my recruit's bags were packed and he was fired.

> I'm hungry! See if Ron wants to go for chicken tonight.

Ty has no love for Tyler Perry, to put it mildly, but Ty is the consummate professional. More importantly, he's the kind of friend who will compliment me when a compliment is deserved, criticize me when criticism is helpful, and if he noticed spinach between my front teeth at a crowded dinner table, he would say so. It is because of his candidness that his take on the *Diary* tour is important to me. Years from now I want to be able to revisit the *Diary* experience from more than just my own perspective. Since the tour is almost over, I thought I'd catch Ty before we both go off to do other things.

We met at a restaurant and laughed and talked about our *Diary* experiences over vegan carrot cake and peach cobbler. The first thing Ty told me is that he'd like nothing more than to have his identity revealed to anyone who ever has the privilege of reading my diary. It will be clear in a couple of paragraphs that *Diary* isn't one of Ty's favorite professional experiences. Ty was blunt about it: He said that he might be broke for a while when the *Diary* tour ends, but if anyone asks him to be in another Tyler Perry production, he'll say no. (Don't believe the "broke" part; maybe Ty doesn't have his next job lined up yet, but he keeps himself a gig.)

I could go on for pages, beginning each sentence with *"Ty said this,"* or *"Ty said that,"* but Ty speaks too well for himself for me to speak for him in the third person. So, I'm going to hand him the pen and let him do his own thing.

DIARY OF A BLACK WOMAN

Memories of a Mad Black Man:
Ty on Tyler

People always ask me why I was not in Tyler Perry's next production and my response is always the same: <u>I am not crazy</u>. Tyler Perry is abusive and he does not give actors room to grow. Even if the abuse is not directed toward you, you are affected because it may be toward a fellow cast member you care about. A cast develops closeness over time, and to see others ripped apart onstage is painful. Like when you hear a 'certain character' ad lib onstage about celebrities such as Whitney Houston, who may have fallen on difficult times. It's not you who's being spoken poorly of, but it's painful nonetheless. In Whitney's case, *she has given us years of good music. If you've ever enjoyed a Whitney song, then instead of kicking her while she's down, you should pray for her to get better. Personally, I think anyone who has something to say about Whitney, who is himself a celebrity, should have his agent contact Whitney's agent and arrange to say it to her face, not to a crowd of strangers.*

I have seen cast members spoken of viciously by Tyler, on and offstage. I saw one nice lady treated so badly that, had it been me, I would have taken every dime of my earnings and given it back to the production company. Madea demeaned that beautiful woman so terribly that everyone felt sorry for her. Another cast member, who was

DIARY OF A BLACK WOMAN

treated well in comparison, was simply referred to as black and stupid—to her face.

Tyler has tried to put down certain women in the cast. He'll take any opportunity he can to use any one of your flaws against you, onstage. In one of Tyler's productions, Madea called a cast member an ugly monkey. Tyler is very nasty to Marva. In the beginning, he was nasty to me because I was hired based on Marva's recommendation. Marva introduced me to the promoter and the promoter hired me directly. He hates that.

Once, when Tyler was supposed to be Madea, he seemed to have forgotten that he's really a man playing a woman, and he became physically aggressive with a real female character onstage. Backstage after the play, the woman was really upset, and told him that he could not be that aggressive with her. He said something like, "I am paying you, blah, blah, blah...." The next day, Tyler apologized. That was one of the nights when Tyler was cocktailing backstage.

At the end of every show, we all come out and take our bows. Tyler has told the audience that his shows do not feature stars like Regina Belle, and that he does not have major pull. He has said that his plays have "no-names" and that he (Tyler) is a success with those no-names. When people in the audience inquire about who we, the cast members are, Tyler pushes us aside. To refer to the cast as "no-names" is an insult. These are fine actors. They deserve recognition. Marva, a couple of other cast members and I are the only ones who do not pucker up and smooch Tyler's derriere. As if his treatment of the cast isn't bad enough, when Tyler gets pissed off with the band, he doesn't even introduce them at the end of the show.

As Madea, Tyler has jumped into other character's love scenes. Why Grandma Madea likes threesomes, I do not know. One time, Madea grabbed a man's crouch onstage. The man had a real-life fiancée who also was in the cast, playing the role of Helen, and Tyler knew it. She and Tyler would fight a lot because Madea would come running in while the lovers were playing their couch scene. If this was a double show day, during the second performance, Helen would say something like, "Hmm, let me see if Madea is going to join us." Tyler especially hates moments like that because the other character, and not Madea, gets the laugh.

There are times when Marva is doing her scenes and Madea will jump in and take her next line and ad lib. Marva stays on track. If Marva improvises and gets a laugh, Tyler will later say that he's the funny one and that Marva shouldn't try to be funny because she's not. Tyler is more interested in being the center of attention than in improving his own production. On top of that, Tyler hates Marva because she is thin and beautiful. He hates her because she's funny. And more than anything, he hates her voice. Tyler wants to sing in the worst way. He's peeved because people are buying Marva's CD.

DIARY OF A BLACK WOMAN

It has been stated in print that Tyler was homeless from time to time. I know that on at least one occasion, Tyler Perry was homeless by choice, that because of certain family circumstances, he chose to live in a car. While I can certainly sympathize with a situation like that, Tyler creates the impression that he was homeless only for the sake of art. He also said that, while working odd jobs, he saved $12,000 and invested it in his first production. I would love to know how he managed to "save" that kind of money, while claiming to be homeless, hungry, and working odd jobs. I wonder if he had any help. Of course, by the time Diary of a Mad Black Woman came along, I know he had access to someone else's money. Along the way, he also did a couple of plays for other producers. My point is not to hate—I'm one to *congratulate, but give credit where it's due, and the investment credit belongs to the investors.*

There was this guy in the production that was all up in Marva's grill, nonstop. It appeared that there was something going on between one of the big wigs and this guy. Now, I'm not one to gossip, but some pictures showed up of the guy, in a bathtub full of bubbles. One of the crewmembers recognized the bathtub as being in the home of...guess who?

One of Marva's love interests in Diary was bisexual and was attracted to her. I think Tyler was told that they were getting too close and got pissed off.

. . .

DIARY OF A BLACK WOMAN

When Marva was new to the Diary set, she really had to focus on adjusting to her role and watching her back. She had a lot deal with. As a seasoned actor, I can afford to pay more attention to what's going on around me. I am one of those people who doesn't take crap off of anyone. Tyler will sometimes have a nip or two before the show, and when he has a cocktail, he's off the chain. There are times when he's really funny. Other times, he will pull power plays. Once, backstage after the show, Tyler decided it would be cute to throw water on people. That was not only immature, but also insane, because there were electrical cables all around. He made the mistake of throwing water on me. I promptly, politely, and efficiently threw an entire bottle of water on Tyler. Everyone assumed that would be my last night in the cast. If that had been the case, it would have been on. Juiced or not, Tyler apparently knew better.

One night, Tyler decided that he wanted to ad lib with me when I was playing a paramedic. He decided that Madea was going to come on to me, sexually. When that happened, I said to Madea, suggestively, 'Oh, is that what you wanna do? Do you want some of this?' Madea chased me offstage. After the show, Tyler said to me, "You nasty bastard...." He went on to comment that, "These [the audience] are good Christian people." The fact is, when you are an actor and someone is constantly coming at you, trying to get a laugh at your expense or trying to steal your scenes, you don't tuck you tail and run away, you go with it. I got the laugh and he didn't like that. He really has a lot of nerve trying to come off like the voice of the Moral Majority. We've seen Madea onstage, butt-naked down to her fat suit. I remember the time when, for no apparent reason, Madea ran naked through the audience while my scene was going on. Tyler will do anything he can to steal your scene.

At one point, Marva took a one-week vacation from Diary that to me felt like a month. While Marva was away, the understudy really messed Helen up. When Marva came back, she really had it; she was the shit. Once Marva truly realized that she was Helen onstage, she was amazing. Everybody was like, "Damn, she got it." You can't just take somebody who has never done theatre and expect them to get it unless you direct them. Tyler never gave Marva any direction. And you don't ad lib with a new cast member who was given a book of dialog to memorize, but Marva was cool with it. She could give it as well as she could take it. With Marva in the play, outside of the fact that this one cast member is a part of Tyler's life, which creates a lot of confusion, we have a really good cast. When Marva's contract is up, I think this production is going to feel her absence.

Since Tyler's name is on the billboard, he acts like he's the king of the cast, on and offstage. Tyler's attitude is, since my name is the only one on the billboard, even offstage, I am going to take advantage of my position. This is my show. I will cut in front of anyone in the food line. I don't fault

DIARY OF A BLACK WOMAN

Tyler for wanting that privilege, but a little politeness and a sense of humor would help. Tyler may be the writer, director, and producer, but he is also a cast member. His attitude doesn't make for a good relationship with the other cast members.

Helen is supposed to be the main character in Diary, and Tyler has a problem with that. When we were taping the Diary video, backstage, everybody said that Marva was performing her scenes really well. That annoyed Tyler so much that he made the video crew cover up the monitors so we couldn't watch anymore. The crew looked at us like, "Is this guy crazy or what!" Tyler was so mad he punched a hole in the wall and starting saying, "I f-----g hate her! I f-----g hate her, f-----g hate her ass." Tyler was so worked up that when it was time for him to go onstage, he slipped and fell.

At the end of our chat, I asked Ty the ultimate question: Was it worth it? Ty responded like a politician: *"We had a lot of fun backstage."*

11

The Remix

Hey Diary,

I just came from work. Same Tyler-Madea crap, different night. Actually, tonight's one of those occasions when I don't know Madea *from* Tyler. Tonight, Tyler was really in a funk. I'm wondering if even he knows who Madea is.

As difficult as it is on a good night, tonight it was painfully hard for me to do the kneeling, groveling, doggie scene. When Helen begs Charles not to leave, he tells her that if she wants him to stay, she should *"bark like a dog."* (Helen is already down on her knees.) I'm a professional and I take pride in my craft. I don't allow myself to cop out, to willingly have bad nights, or even bad scenes, so I proceeded to bark like the script requires. But, for a moment, I thought about lunging forward and taking a plug out of Charles' leg. I can just see it: first, the shock on Charles' face, then the panic as he tries to shake Helen off his leg.

> *If my handwriting gets scraggly, it's because I'm on the floor dying laughing right now.*

There is no mention of what kind of dog Helen's supposed to be. In an opinion poll, most people would probably say a poodle. But naw, the Helen I've conjured up is a pit bull, so my teeth are locked onto Charles' leg. Charles is singing his

DIARY OF A BLACK WOMAN

big solo number, but in my imagined version of the play, right about now, the acting stops. The actor stops singing, and starts screaming. The audience thinks it's all part of the script and women are on their feet screaming, *"Bite him, bite him!"* Not one to be upstaged, instead of Tyler putting on his director's hat and ordering the crew to close the stage curtain momentarily, Madea comes onstage with a fake can of mace and tries to mace Helen. Helen lets go of Charles and, still on all fours, chases Madea offstage.

Tonight, for just one night, I would have loved to bring to the stage a woman with a spine, to offer up my own rewrite of my character. Sort of like a remix. I probably should explain what a "remix" is. Musically, a remix is a new production of an existing song. If I were to rewrite the Helen character, there are a few things I would do differently. Hmm, this could be fun. It would be interesting to contrast the script as Tyler wrote it with scenes where Helen steps out of character and speak directly to the audience, creating her own remix scenes, saying something different and funny, then returns to the original script and delivers most of the line as Tyler wrote it. (Actually, I do sort of step out of character from time to time, but never as extremely as I'd like to.) While this is happening, the other characters onstage would freeze. Helen would face the audience and say something along the lines of, *"Wait a minute. Let me show you how to do this."* The other characters would resume the script where they left off, but Helen would become neo-Helen and do and say something entirely different. I'm not trying to rewrite Tyler's play. I just want to change Helen's responses here and there because of the abuse she takes from Charles. After all, this is a comedy; why shouldn't Helen steal scenes and get laughs? Here are some examples:

Charles' Big Vocal Number
After Charles tells Helen he's not happy, and that he's leaving, he breaks out into his big vocal number, a song entitled *Didn't Wanna Tell You*. He's singing his heart out, mouth opened wide enough to see his lungs. While Charles sings, Helen is on the other side of the living room, looking sad.

. . .

The Remix
Helen calls Tyler onstage. Charles, who had frozen, comes back to life and resumes his wide-mouthed singing. When he hits a long, high note, Helen produces a toilet plunger from underneath the sofa and shoves it onto Charles' face. Charles' singing becomes muffled, yet he continues to sing, seemingly unaware that he's sucking a toilet plunger.

Homebody
Helen is depicted as a homebody who spends her time performing domestic chores, wearing outfits straight out of an episode of *One Life to Live*.

The Remix
As Charles leaves out the front door to go to work, Helen is seen shedding her signature green robe.

Underneath, she's wearing tight, low cut black leather pants and a halter top. Timing her exit perfectly, as Charles walks out the front door, Helen winks at the audience then slithers out the back door.

Working Late
Charles claims he has to work late. Helen's response to the news is whining and whimpering.
<u>The Remix</u>
When Charles delivers his usual lie, Helen walks over to Charles, slaps him dead in the mouth, and says, *"Don't you lie to me!"*

My Old "New" Man
Helen first encounters Orlando, her future love interest, when he delivers a package to her home.

Helen's father-in-law, Daddy Charles (Tyler Perry) says Orlando is a nice man and that Helen should hook up with him. Helen chides Daddy Charles for even suggesting such a thing.

The Remix

Helen says to the audience: *"Puleeze! I've been hitting that since the first time he handed me a package; and believe you me, it was a 'special delivery'."*

The Accident

When Helen learns that Charles has had a terrible accident, her reaction is, *"I hope he rots in hell."*

The Remix

Helen speaks directly to the audience, hands on hips, neck moving side-to-side, sistah style, and says, *"What accident? I paid GOOD money to have that fool ran off the road."*

That was fun! Needless to say, I like the remixed lines a whole lot better. The problem, of course, is that Helen gets the laughs. Tyler would never go for that.

12

The End

Dear Diary,

Well, for me, the tour is over; my contract ended today. Needless to say, there was drama to the end. As for me, I'm going into the studio to record a new CD, written and co-written, with the help of a few talented people, by Marva King. Produced by Marva King for Marvalous Works Entertainment, Inc. After all the control others have attempted to exert over me, I need to be in charge. I'm going to miss writing; it was one of the best things that came out of *Diary*. I hope to publish my diary to encourage other women to take charge of their lives. Even when we don't control the big picture, we should not to let the individual scenes control us.

Hopefully, things will go smoothly and I can give the old pen a break, but who knows, I may have to write again soon. You see, there's this producer who's been winking at me when he's not winking at this male background singer with long '70s sideburns and a full beard....Just kidding.

Peace.

Note from the Author

Where Am I Now?

I am happy to report that I'm just completing an eight month promotional tour for my CD, *Light of Day*. I had a lot of fun performing and meeting wonderful new people and spending time with friends and acquaintances in and outside the United States. Although I'm a recent newcomer to the film industry, I have a few credits: I'm featured in *Resurrection: The J.R. Richard Story*, scheduled for a 2005 release; I will be featured in two films slated to begin production in 2005—one titled *B.M.W.*, and another as yet untitled film. I am preparing to record a new CD titled "*Soul Sistah*" consisting of R&B and old school soul music. My upcoming CD is dedicated to Sly Stone and all of the pioneer soul, blues, R&B and jazz artists who were successful in status but robbed of their monetary treasures. I will do a major city tour in support of the CD. I have a teenage son who I am assisting while he attends a music conservatory. Expect to hear great things from him. Along with some other writers I am developing some ideas for stage and television productions. Y'all look out!

Oh, I almost forgot: I'm featured on a Brazilian and American jazz CD titled *Soul of Brazil* scheduled for release in 2005. It's smooth and hot, hot, hot! I could mention a whole lot more, but I'm sure you get the idea: I'm not sitting around twiddlin' my thumbs. I am truly blessed and thankful. I give all praise to my Lord and Father above.

By the way, rumors that I "quit the business" have been circulating for quite some time. I have not quit the business; I only quit the *Diary* production, and for good cause. Had I not done so, I wouldn't have furthered my own ventures.

Marva King

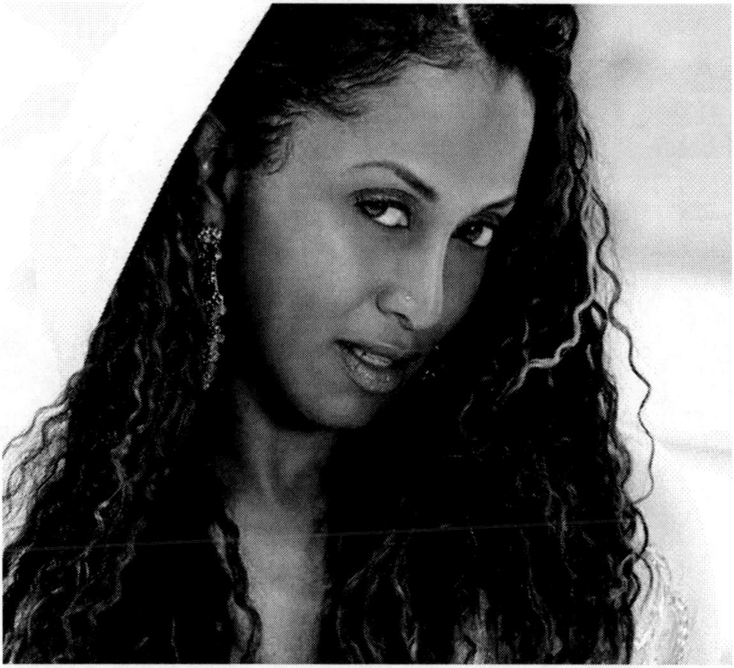

Questions

What is your opinion of Helen? Did you consider the character to be realistic?

How would you have reacted to Charles' treatment if you were Helen?

_____
_____
_____
_____
_____
_____
_____
_____
_____
_____
_____
_____
_____

Do you feel it was wrong for Helen to leave Charles in the shower? Could you forgive your mate for the type of cruelty exhibited by Charles?

_____
_____
_____
_____
_____
_____
_____
_____
_____
_____
_____
_____

How would you react if your best friend had an affair with your boyfriend or your husband? Who would you be most angry at: your friend or your mate? Why?

What advice would you give your daughter if she were married to a man like Charles?

Helen got on her knees and "barked like a dog" in an effort to keep her man. How far have you or would you go to maintain a relationship?

_____
_____
_____
_____
_____
_____
_____
_____
_____
_____
_____
_____

Charles offered financial security; Orlando offered respect and affection. Which would you have chosen? Would you have left Charles for Orlando?

_____
_____
_____
_____
_____
_____
_____
_____
_____
_____
_____
_____
_____

Check out my new CD, *Soul Sistah*, in stores or on the worldwide web.

www.marvaking.com